# needlegrass

Also by Dennis Sampson:


*The Double Genesis*
*Forgiveness*
*Constant Longing*

# needlegrass

dennis sampson

Carnegie Mellon University Press
Pittsburgh 2005

Acknowledgments

Grateful acknowledgment is made to the editors of the following journals in which some of these poems first appeared, at times in different versions:

*The Black Warrior Review, The Greensboro Review, The Hudson Review, Pequod, Third Coast,* and *Traffic East.*

The author extends his gratitude to the Virginia Arts Commission and the North Carolina Arts Council for grants in 1997 and 2001. For their help with this book, thanks go to my friends Larry Hamlin and Louie Skipper.

Book design: Kristen Romonovich

The publication of this book is supported by a grant from the Pennsylvania Council on the Arts.

Library of Congress Control Number 2003112552
ISBN 0-88748-418-2

Printed and bound in the United States of America

10  9  8  7  6  5  4  3  2  1

# Contents

FIVE

for my sisters, Karen and Linda


*. . . of following the flight of the bee*
*without being able to calculate*
*which way—of seeing cattle mate—*
*of sequence and consequence and arrangement. . . .*
*I think of that first place again*
*now close enough to touch—now far away.*

For The Dawn


What comes to me now comes slowly
and I am alone
with the death of everyone
I have known, with my daughter
dressed as if for a wedding
in the dark of this first morning,
this first night,
my oldest sister in silence
outside the door that will not open
until time is no longer time
and the heavens fall.

It is the ocean
before the sun, the waste of water
borne through the night,
that lets the beginning
and the end become finally
what I can fathom. The face of a god
crumbles to fine dust.
My love of a woman disperses
like seed through the air.
One star steadies itself.
It goes out. Now I am no one.

And the sound of the waves
is the sound of the shameless
chasing after what never was.
Water to green water. Give me
the heedless world again.
Come toward me, mustard weed.
My own heart stops hurrying.
More than the sun. More than the light.

I wear the ladder of sky,
a bare tree twisting upward
like the still flame

gliding slowly back to me now
lighter,
meadow of lupine, gorge of black rock.

My father finds peace.
My mother weeps in the dawn.
And it is final
and it is beginning
in this place below the dark.

# ONE

*Lie upon your own bed, commune with your own heart,*
*and be still.*

—Psalm 4

## Silent Witness

After he turns off the light he lies awake in the dark remembering
his childhood. Hard to believe that he moved through the fields
under the wide sky of the plains just north of Pierre, South Dakota,
and saw the geldings grazing the far hills
  overlooking the valley. Mist at dawn is sheared off by the breeze.

It becomes a gale, bends the needlegrass in one direction . . . and he
is running along a fenceline, his shirt in his hand, then up the ridge
in the shadow of a cloud that follows him into the smell of clover.
Stops, is still. His eyes fill with a seeing not their own.
  The other side of the highway the white screen of the drive-in

faces the sun across blue heaven. Hard to believe, covered in
a blanket shared with his sisters, that he stared and stared
at *The Man Who Shot Liberty Valance* flashing across that screen
on the fifth of July while the disembodied voice of
  Jimmy Stewart crackled from the speaker hung from the window.

Now and then the aroma of his father's cologne washes over
the odor of popcorn, and in his heart he stops. That man.
That woman. And he sees his mother's face in the radiance
and he leans—her soft cheek glowing—to rest his small arms
  upon the seat, his chin on his hand, wanting to be in that world

of one woman and one man so much different from the one he is
now living in. Images: He takes them one at a time, turns them over
as if they were a precious gemstone between forefinger and thumb
in the light of a jeweler's glass.
  His father, after putting on his hat in the hallway, hesitates

before the oval mirror. He is studying his appearance, this man
who never seemed to care about what clothes he should wear;
and for an instant his father seems to know who he is. Readjusts
his hat, is satisfied, goes out, comes back in. He has forgotten
  his wallet. His keys. His checkbook. I would like to witness

this man again through the eyes of a child, arranging the reeds
of his clarinet on the bed. The polyester pants, the shirt sleeves
rolled up to the elbow, the gratitude expressed during every meal,
"This tastes good, Lu. Especially the meatloaf."
  Then the boy is down the hill with a stick snapped

from a honey locust along the rim of the valley. Cattle spill
from the plains to feed in the shadow of late afternoon. One of them
looks up as if to puzzle out what this might mean—the equation
is difficult. Goes back to grazing. There is a chill,
  the breeze that blew warmly pours through leaves of the aspen

and sweat dries on the boy's neck. He thinks: Be careful. Break
an ankle and they might not find you for days. Thinks: You'll be
devoured by the beasts of the night, the fox giving way
to the coyote after the fierce defense. Watch
  for the diamondback withdrawing to its monastery under a rock,

coiled in cool dirt, listening.

★★★

The rattlesnake, the wind, this night too, with its wild geometry
of stars spiraling westward over the river, the night that takes
in everything from the flowering cactus to the expanse of avenues,
carless after midnight,
  the cottonwoods and lawns still and dark outside his house.

Night, that suddenly changes the roses closing up along the porch:
night and the wind. And the scent of something unidentifiable
drawn from a long way off that reaches my open window
where I lie weaving a path through what is lost,
  cupping my hands in the creek, the frigid pureness dripping

from my chin that makes the muscles of my throat contract,
kneeling in sand, hunger sated again and again at the kitchen table,
then up alongside the Missouri River six blocks from my front steps,

that served as silent witness to everything that mattered
   that couldn't be expressed. The fragrance of my father's Mennen.


Jimmy Stewart pulls back on the reins and slides from his saddle
to confront his nemesis, dressed in black leather.
My youngest sister's hand from the distance of forty years
grips my wrist. Guns go off. Jimmy Stewart is left
   standing. "If you could live your life over," Karen asks


one night out of nowhere, "what would you do different?"
"What are you talking about?" father answers. "Go back to bed."
And the sun descends across the long horizon, suffusing the clouds
with scarlet and calming the meadowlark,
   perplexed on a fence post. Its song is elegiac. Tentative. Shadows


darken the lawns and twilight changes to night again long after
the morning dove along the limits of the city starts with its haunting
song. See. Accept what you see. Your sisters talking in bed. Your
mother rolling her nylons from ankle
   to thigh, her immaculate hands. Your sisters sit cross-legged,


facing each other now. They are telling stories that keep them up
long after everyone else has gone to sleep. There is the story
of the hermit who hung himself with his belt in a ramshackle shed
built into a hill, the story
   of the receptionist with jet-black hair who married a pharmacist


because he came with money and who by slow degrees went out
of her mind. One day she never appeared again. The story
of the ghost in the willow, in the attic under the crescent
moon, in the graveyard,
   in the lake—the ghost that floated up out of a man's chest


and groomed itself in the bureau mirror, trailing its forefinger
along the arm of a chair, with green eyes, wanting to come back
to this dark world, drifting into the kitchen. The ghost
in the window that studied you
   long after you had turned away. Song of the cricket. Song

of the wind. Someone is whistling in the kitchen. What's that tune?
What is it? Father is preparing a sandwich of egg salad and rye.
He stops whistling when he can't remember where he put his knife.
*Strangers on the Shore.* A riff from
  Benny Goodman. "What are you eating now?" my mother asks

from the sofa. "A little egg salad sandwich. I don't know why I'm
so hungry." A man and a woman lie down in the night for fifty years,
he with the radio playing, she with her face to the wall with wide
open eyes. The smell of one is indistinguishable
  from the other. It is the smell of the river—the smell of rain on dirt,

of blizzards. Of cut grass. Through the dining room window
shadows thrash. They have a story too. All shall be well, all
manner of things—all in good time. Now go on living, say
those shadows.
  And there is joy in that, and there is pain.

# Midnight Of The Word

Hawks ride high above the prairie, circling, circling, and as the prelude
to the thunderstorm wind, along with the sudden dark, drives birds
to their nests and brings men running out to their cars to close
the windows. Then quietness, the wind is listening—
   then that brilliant whip of lightning that summons you out

of the house looking there, then there—the second flash caught
out of the corner of your eye. It is high summer. And your uncles
drink Storz beer from their steins, burping and smoking in the den.
"We need this rain," Uncle Harlan offers philosophically,
   and the others nod. Then lightning shakes the world again. Feel

the reverberation stutter up through the foundation of the house,
up through your legs. Peer out the window into the street stunned
by the stillness of maples faintly illuminated, quivering. North
Riverview is dreaming, the whole city in a vast
   communal sleep that suggests you are the only one up in the world,

that for this protracted moment in front of the latticed pane
what you think is significant, the voyeur at ten turning over notions
vaguely ontological. That time might be suspended. That the lamp
left on in a single house implies a crushing loneliness, and within
   this hovering stillness that asks for nothing, nor settles for less,

a disposition of spirit lives. Back through years and everything comes
down to your silhouette at the window in your pajamas, against which
the unshakable feeling of separateness is measured. In the dusk
above the yellow blossoms of the four o'clocks, sphinx moths
   manuever, a blur of wings drawing nectar, in delicate hesitation.

They fling themselves in a violent arc against the dark and are gone.

★★★

And I come quietly forth reaching out my hand, long after my mind
has won this truth for me, readjusting my palm around each flower,
withdrawing it after the moths have rocketed away, lifting it
at their return. One is cupped. Nothing fights harder, a racket
  within both hands, my palms pressed closer to quiet what shows

its head just above the knuckle of the thumb. In summer
a murmuring. Then a hush. Soft wind. A car door shuts. One bird
continues somewhere on the other side of Bonnie Robinson's garden,
continucs insistently
  as if to say the end of this day is not acceptable—as if to call those

who know better back—no one persuaded by its singing. The half
moon rides through the sky showcasing a ballet of mosquito hawks
high above the houses—whose lights have all come on—
then lower so one can almost make out,
  in last light, their markings. Whoever looks up knows

this lifting of one's eyes to behold the night and its several stars,
knows this lying on the grass with one's hands entwined
as the occasional meteor burning itself out across the cosmos,
knows this cloud passing before
  the moon directly overhead, as neither far nor near, here

nor elsewhere, spelling out in images what stitches the seasons
together, etching a splay of wrinkles at the edge of a father's eyes,
rots the molar, shudders a wave of gold across the prairie while
enticing a purple wildflower fringed with magenta
  up from a crack in the abandoned parking lot. In secret it searches,

unhurriedly, as if to proclaim: This is just one life, and death
puts out the light in the housefly, the bullsnake skidded over,
twisting—one final irrelevant flick—the caterpillars in their nests
in the cottonwood gone up in flames
  and my father standing back flipping open and closed the silver

lid of his lighter. Lean nearer.

# TWO

## To My Friend In Need

You had a life. There was wind and rain
stripping the Bradford pear tree of its blossoms
the afternoon your ex-wife
suddenly remarked how much she liked to draw
when she was a child. There were blue jays too,
getting after a hawk above your house.
You watched, stepping away from a son
until you lost your balance in the driveway.
There was fire in winter. Frost on a field of poppies.
Deep canyons where the red-tail dropped to night.

You had the touch. It wasn't as awful as you thought
cupping a mother's fragile hands
while she spoke in detail of her first husband
shot down over Italy the last day of the war,
the palomino giving his great neck to you
along the fenceline off Chickasa Road,
dipping its head when you stopped
just that moment—what a wonder that was.
Someone made figure eights into your arms
when you closed your eyes. That was a daughter

pushing off onto the ice under tall lights
and gliding, calling you to follow her into the dark.
Then you cherished the severed appendages
of old sculptures, gardens left unrevised,
the expression on a stranger's face rising out
of Mallard Lake, delighted to have swum so far—
that Baptist church in Andalusia gutted by fire.
You wanted a companion. You were given study
of the long field, geese over plains at twilight
What you craved never kept you from loving

what you got. Now, in the dark,
nothing to do in a house where the white-
throated sparrow at seven o'clock twice utters
its devastating song, recall how you straddled
the body of a man on his back in 1995 to give
him back to life, breathing repeatedly into his
mouth with the supplication "Get up, get up"
from behind. Thank God you had the good sense
to see how lucky you had become. You had a life.
Now you see you could not love it enough.

## Childhood Bible

Grackle, undertaker, mourner, bore,
the only book so solemn you are never stolen,
nitpicked by Jehovah's Witnesses in starched
white shirts straddling Schwinns, pressed close to the breast,
shaken above the stupendous hairpiece of the evangelist
and scoured by my brother-in-law for phrases
that might justify the hatred he felt for himself.
What brings you back like Lazarus this afternoon
to my eyes that have looked inward for so long?

Every now and then I took you down
to flip through the rules of Leviticus then turned
to the maps in the back: nothing made sense.
What was all the fuss? Why did my sister
lay open the pages of the Psalms on my pillow
then never say anything, as if I'd done
something hideous that must never be discussed?
And why years later did Doctor Lavender,
lover of cheap sherry and the blasphemous answer,
slip you inside his travel bag before surgery
when he thought I wasn't looking? Heavy
in the hand, as if soaked in honey, crimson
along the rim, you were a serious presence
—grim sentinel among all other texts.

The Sickle Moon


Put him there with the mailman
   crushing a black widow with his thumb.
Put him with the mother whose son
   stole into a neighbor's home when the family was gone
and danced before the mirror
   in a daughter's clothes until he was caught,
shaming his father
   into moving to Minneapolis that September.


   Put him with the photographer
screamed out of his house after midnight
   by a wife as wildly withdrawn
as the woman he would read about that fall
   in Charlotte Bronte's novel,
beautiful, hysterical, and laconic,
   with Murphy Mullins who taught biology
and fathered a stillborn child
   in secret with Eleanor Gregory,
rushing it out to the dump where it was found,
   one hand lifted out of the rubble,


with the village misanthrope that came to the Hopscotch Bar
   just once to watch the stripper twist,
with the owner of McCracken's
   Lawn and Shrub so amiable and tall
and always there with a joke,
   struck by lightning because he thought not to work
in a thunderstorm
   was unforgivable. Put him there with the daughter
in shock at the wake,
   wide-eyed and infuriated and unable
to look into the coffin,
   with the minister who seemed so peculiar
at Piggly Wiggly in Bermuda shorts
   reading a tabloid, with the kid
whose father embezzled thousands,

watering flowers
outside his house—in exile from us.

    Put him there with the misery
of tight-lipped women turning to sleep
    as their last resort on a night
when the sickle moon above
    the Presbyterian steeple shines,
inquiring of a child who someday will be forced
    to remember it all.

Loving Women


I used to run my palms along their long faces
so I could feel the monumental sorrow of those gods,
great grandmothers golden
in late light letting themselves be caressed,
Ellen, the night nurse, the seamstress under the tree, Doreen,

small enough to get my arms around
out there by herself in the prairie
trying so hard to sing with the meadowlark,
clearing her throat. Memory allows
a sapling now to sprout from her jagged mouth,

and the dance moves of Fred Astaire and Ginger Rogers,
in acknowledgment of this sincerest thought
made visible, come to a stop. I see
a black ant making its way erratically
to the very tip of that tongue and hear it speak

to the multitude—the crickets, along with the bullfrogs—
with prayer, then with quiet beseeching.
Bless their fidelities, their rough edges,
their lemonades, their aching backs
and clean sheets: Aunt Beverly, Arlyce and Darleen.

They waited so long for this to be said
of what is best in me.

## The Meaning That Eludes The Life You're Living

I believe you have to be unhappy
to go back to the girl in the green dress
eating an apple during recess,
her legs spread wide on the steps
of Bradford Elementary the last
day of class—to find the meaning that eludes
the life you're living. You want back
the sense of something exquisite about
to begin: that girl taking long
pauses between one crunch and another,
her green dress to her knees,
revealing the mystery of underpants.

The skirt of a young girl in the wind—
her slip rippling then at rest,
one fold fluttering—reminds you this is a beginning
you can live with. Let her go on savoring
the taste of a Granny Smith apple,
bored with other girls in a dance of Ring
Around the Roses. That's it.
That's all there is, which you have
to have. If you are not convinced
ask that girl in sunlight,
spitting what's soft and rotten into her hand.

# In August Just After Sunrise

Suddenly the great buck in the tallgrass stops, raises its head,
glances back apprehensively over miles of silence.
It begins to graze. The others are strung out along the glistening bluff

in what seems a weightless wandering—
a mirage. Their coloring is the coloring of straw

and when the sun has hung in the sky above the arroyo
for a while they become a nothingness shifting beneath the eye intent
on finding what otherwise can't be wrung
from the faithless world—a story in any tongue.

★ ★ ★

Once, when the squall steered north over the draw there was a hush,
a prolonged calm encouraging me to come closer.
The youngest female draped her long slender throat over the neck

of another, resting there. And I heard a *crack*
sending them bolting over ridges of laurel, a bullet just above the
buck's front thigh, hitting
with a thud,
and it whipped itself wildly to one side. In that summer sun

I watched the hunter rise, then stand quite still,
the pronghorns
long gone into stands of pine . . .
and I turned to observe that cautious coming forward,

how, pausing to peer above the needlegrass on his toes,
he let his rifle drop and
circled that beast struggling
to get up. With one savage hand he pulled away and up with his knife.

Not once did I take my eyes off.

★ ★ ★

Now I come again in August just after sunrise
in love with the solitude

of sleek creatures borne effortlessly over prairie grass turning lush
after long rain.

        There, where the river widens, bordered
with sunflowers and sweet clover and sage, the pronghorns graze again

then vanish with the wind's
perceptible ebb and flow—through rippling bluestem. They too have
forgotten

        and have come back gladly with their lives. They raise their heads
to look
in my direction
in this story that does not stop.

# THREE

Eden


Not a care in the world
caressing the winged limb of the ash.
Or crouching to chart the path of the black ant.
The iridescent spectacle of wasps
coupling in mid-air above the white impatiens
is touched on by the light—
huge ferns     dogwoods     tulips opening wide
chickadees   blue birds   wrens
everywhere an assertion of singleness.

But it is the symmetry of Eden
surrounded by a gate that can't be located,
curvature and line—motif and theme—
that haunts me when I have lost my way
in the loud world: configuration of snow geese
up which one dreams. Give me
cattle winding back from the pasture,
patterns of the newly created long-
stemmed wildflowers flashing their deep red,
the smell of rain in high cedars.

Dark stones cloaked in algae
glitter beneath the irritable surface of a stream.
And after a while the principle of analogy
is ruthlessly borne upward into
crystalline eyes, the wind
seems like the night sky coming at you,
one thing another in ways bewitching—how,
watching the Indigo Bunting sip
from the cleft in a rock,
loyalty of water to thirst occurs,
night's oneness closes round.
Then maybe the craving to love what can't

be loved without the experience
of evil—the river that speaks of time
in a timeless region. The cricket underfoot
shakes off its death. The resurrected silkworm

goes humpbacked along the lip
of a leaf. Wounds close. No one suffers.
There is no place for sorrow in the heart.
And yet what passes on wide wings
remains, and what's to come
wakes Adam in his bed of straw,
not knowing what to make of his
first reverie along a river
coursing through columbine and sage,
his eyes looking into eyes for what was there
just yesterday—the realization of age,
wind scented with imminent snow.

Linger underneath the silhouette of a great tree with me.
Consider how meaningless its gesticulations
without the hint of decrepitude conveyed.
It is the symmetry of Eden,
distribution of the various and the same,
order beyond the argument for order
that fevers me, the beautiful made more beautiful
because the metaphor looms, like *low mist creeping*
season upon season upon season.
Night like the mind. Like blinding insight
light strikes the wave, and grief
seeks its equivalent in towering cypresses
bent hard away from Eden. Someone is fashioning a key

for which no lock exists
until a fiercer vision intervenes.
It is the first decision, Eve,
the dread of life inspired by the rhetoric
of a snake stretched out in lassitude
beneath a veil of leaves.

At night the memory that I make
of getting up at dawn to sit
with my asthmatic sister, counting the minutes,
of following the flight of the bee
without being able to calculate
which way—of seeing cattle mate—
of sequence and consequence and arrangement . . .
I think of that first place again
now close enough to touch—now far away.

Autumn And Age, River And Time

Who would have thought divinity would be nothing more
than this evening's shadow,
the death of Linda Kaulda across the street,
on fire, flailing and screaming before the sun had risen

—in spring the delicate narcissus
—in autumn the descent of
a leaf caught in your palm to the applause of those who would always
love you?

Linda, I remember, just a kid.

This was all part of the story,
the feminine tuft of dandelion lifted to your lips
blown free of its stem,
the sun a vivid resurrection of yellow coming up over the thunderhead,

that passionate glance that turns the afterlife to salt
making you wish
you were a single maple out on the prairie beginning to spin.

I see this shadow in that passing shine, poised as it was
the summer my mother danced
with an obliging broom to the tune of *Strangers On the Shore* and
my father lifted me

out of my chair with a wild saxophone.
In the years
of going alone along a road, I saw that shadow as beautiful . . .

*Alone, alone,* the cricket questioned me,
reiterating its sole song—the bullfrog's flagrant baritone.
Listening now the strangeness of these soloists
struck me: *You are a miracle of one.*

And deep-rooted in my growing dark I retraced
my steps, to walk among fathers towering in their happiness.

If You Were Here

Let me tell you how the wind
in the summer drought withered the sumac beside the chain-link
fence
and whisked the clouds away. They came back
again and again. There were enough clouds for us all.

How one night I turned on the light outside the porch
and it lit just half the suffering mulberry
bent and reaching upward with its fingertips touching
the full moon. It seemed skeletal, beautiful. A ghost.

I was alone. But I never lost the feeling of being watched
by what was compassionate—thus my mumbled
conversations sitting in my Adirondack chair outside as the sun
rushed up. The dawn: impossible to believe I missed it for one month.

Sorrow. There was sorrow. The first snow stained my heart
because I wasn't ready for that gentleness,
the inner transformation mocked by flakes that flew.
How did that happen so suddenly when I worked so hard?

I can identify for you the various weeds, read the minds of flowers,
show how the liturgy of the cardinal
exemplifies that love is nearly enough. It never is.
For once the world can't be betrayed by the beautiful lie.

Elegy For The Rest Of The World

Take that man back again to swaying weeds
where a barefooted woman stares down happily
from a picnic table at a heart cut in the grass
and wind is still the mystery of this world's being,

to what curved effortlessly inward and away
like the fantasies of a kid with stars in his blue eyes
who found at the gate the dragon
guarding the impatient princess alone in her high tower.

Nothing of the kind was called upon
by anyone but him to search
who had come so far to see her rest her eyes upon his face.

Take him back to the barbed wire fence flecked with feathers
and clover along a prairie, to the small face in the window
turned away from the page of a diary in childish script,

to Miles played along the night of fireflies
and one red light going on and off in the distance.

There he can stand forever in the shape of a mulberry
satisfied by this wind that shifts
after midnight and moves through everything
like a finger twisting a single strand of black hair,

not expecting anything of anyone
who has given him every wish that she were there.

Heedless World

   Death left us at the threshold. We expected more.
      Night wind,
have your way with giant foxtail. Frost
   with yellow brome—blight with chokecherry.

   Black nightshade,
you with your dozen forbidden berries,
      you flourish.
   You persist. Still misanthrope of the prairie.

   Blue wind,
you are where the scent of river water is
      even to the man
   who does not understand what he loves.

      Heron,
   you are flashing underneath the harvest moon.

   Crow, you are descending
into the bent mulberry, the sycamore, lighting on the ground,
      your uproar over nothing
   forgotten just as the sun goes down.

   Aster,
you are where you won't be noticed
      along the meadow's edge.
   I know, you are giving yourself again to the brown field.

   Light, you warm the water meadow,
heighten the veins of the leaf, then pull back.
      You are where daisy fleabane
turns her white face to you. You are shining.

## A Tree In Childhood, Long Since Taken Down

It is still there when I pass,
the two parting boughs flung upward
like the arms of the devoted
during that most passionate moment
at a revival, tent billowing in the wind.
They are praising the evangelist of the abyss.
Absence. It is almost presence.
It is loss. You cannot capture
what vanished into the phantoms
you now live with of sisters refusing
to climb down. Their laughter's
a trickle of bliss ground finally to silence.

The truth is the interlude and what
it leads to, and even the conclusion's
overcome by simply living
through it: two wives, three children
strange to you. Nude,
the woman you loved opened her long slender legs
and gave you something additional to lose.
One funeral. Change is cruel.
But remember in silhouette last September
her getting out of bed to look for a minute
for a book that was not there?
Who we are. Who we will turn into.

Let that live oak represent
what slipped through the fingers and be
a symbol for the disappearance of dark
feminine eyes looking directly, relentless,
the taste of a woman's mouth in bed at Christmas
opened over yours—what it means to be human.
Brutal. But what is there to do?
Then the oak begins in the wind to move.

# FOUR

The Blessing Of Silence Bestowed

          The one about the oncologist
in his eighties after open-heart surgery
saying he couldn't recall one single meaningful day,
the anorexic beautician reeking of perfume

with her back to the cafeteria,
and what you have to live with in a trailer
set back in the woods with the stench of the refinery
in your hair. I draw the curtain

and stop on my way to the door in the dark and feel
the spirit I've known. In silence
God seems to forgive the swindler
sitting down with his wife and kids

at the end of the day, the adulteress—the killer.
And I too experience the bliss
shuddering up my spine and spilling
along this dream that humbles me.

Let yourself witness
what graces the baby with golden locks
then turns the hurricane out to sea,
soothes and simplifies—weeps for the unbeliever.

Don't look away for an instant,
mercy and memory finding a place to rest, a place to rave:
the argument for misery
along with the argument for having lived.

## April Snow

I came upon your photograph again and followed
what used to be, a forbidden gesture
to be recorded in the ledgers
of the deities—along with that woman's turning
to look back at a burning tower
and the lyricist that just could not help himself.

The park shuts down in a solitude of snow.
Even those bold flowers,
daylilies all, which set out in November to say
again who they are,
withdraw like bridesmaids into a deeper interior
we can never know.

You were beautiful. The long candles lit
on the mantlepiece, you prepared an altar
for the sacrifice that started
with your stepfather hitting your sister in the mouth
and ended in a fall of snow.
I loved the essential sorrow of your story.

I don't want to write poetry anymore,
that wild performance
of getting dressed to the nines to witness the wedding
of light and dark. This is for those spoken
for—by the flute and the lyre.
They come up breathless. They are turned to salt.

What The Human Voice Is For

One summer
in a theater in Cleveland,
during a scene in a movie I can't recall
where Burt Reynolds was being punished,
he put out his hands,
spread wide to show all ten fingers
to his torturer,
while a cluster of teenagers twittered and guffawed
until a man in the back shouted
"There is nothing funny about suffering
so shut up."
Then silence, the silence of the saved,
then the tease
of waiting for one of those kids to say
what he would regret.
I remember the strength
I took from that,
that I understood what the human voice
was for.

So why is it this hard to ask one simple blessing
nights when I am driven to the edge
by what I could have done
if only I had been someone other than who I am?

I want the soul to be a fragrance
of pine and wind
before the storm. Let it pass
through what in me remains betrayed.
I want the soul to know
and lead me there.

Obit


To die. It was simply a matter of lying down
after circling like a dog until just the right moment,
waiting for that wave far out to sea at dusk
to pour over my final thought—
laved and lightened and lifted out of this life.

What more do you want? An encomium?
That the white moth
that fluttered up and into my blue eyes that night
might show how fickle fortune was?
That my love of the unobtainable be crushed?

That in middle life gravity became a monster
while I walked through the day
without the slightest notion of who I would become.

That the wing of the moth
underneath the lamp that illuminated the tiny lies
I tried to describe might be uncorrupted
by the hand that steered it outward into the night.

That I wanted to die.
That something be said of what I loved.

# What The Rising Of The Dead Shall Mean

1.

The dead will not rise up in their coffins.
They will not die again.

You will never see them cooking in a circle
nor hear at twilight a ruckus to wake the living.

The dead will not hover the half-lit houses
nor carry the wind along.

They will not bless their fathers
and mothers who are endeared to them.

The dead are indifferent to the dead.
They are indifferent to women in dark dresses.

Though you bow before them
the dead do not move.

Though you decorate their graves
the dead do not move.

The dead will not follow you through your room.
They will not sing to you when you are alone.

The dead do not remember who you are.
They do not dream of coming back to you.

2.

      UNCLE HARLAN THAT NOVEMBER DAY
riding a light through the sky
      somewhere back in a time turned darker for the years.

    And the voice learned from the earth,
intones, from the grit of listening shale:

*Mine is the silence of an oak remembering all down*
*its trunk to the dry dirt of summer*

*the first leaf of its making,*
*down through the massive root,*

*the black marl, the molten lava.*

*Mine is a meditation of stone turned to earth,*
*earth to grit.*

What you have come to is a note,
the names of the long dead marveling

the moment of creation when the voices tremble together

into a single utterance
only time can obliterate, cough from another millennium,
cry,

your uncle's laughter
inhabiting a landscape of blown wheat,
sworn to secrecy by the people who would not have it any other way.

3.

The labor of my father's hands by which
a world grew up
around him
disappears with that simple song moaned out,

and I am listening to the words that have meaning
for me only if the wind quits,
the night looms darker, his lips whispering through the past.

I have seen the dead during that hour of mourning
and that hour of joy,
incipient illumination eked out of the fingertip, squeezed,

light from the first light,
the image arranged within a halo of human feeling.

       In that backward glance,
in memory's splendid misunderstanding
    of time and space,
            look in your isolation,
in your first yearning,

     for the Great Bear, find Pegasus, Orion. Find un-
created night, repeated patterns of felicity

    woven by a needle stitching the universe,
the sunflower fringed with black still bearing up under the weight
    of a million years.

       UNCLE HARLAN THAT NOVEMBER DAY
and the cocoon cracked open, starved and fallen into my palm.

   It releases me,
a liberation of sandstone wall, meadowlark, mournful dove,

fragrance of bluestem where the nighthawk nests.
    And my father comes forward
in the needlegrass, head tilted as if curious, and the listening begins:

     *Someone is waiting*

   *beyond the hill     beyond deep shade*
     *of a great tree where horses drop their dung*
  *in the long grass, swinging their manes    Run*

   *because you must     past sunflowers    past Denson's meadow*
     *through the alder grove   it's closer*
   *than you think   it's right here*
               *Cattle graze*

        And I can trace that rhythm
where I stand,
        that chant married to the movement of bare feet

        when it is noon,
when it has come to night: cold stars, root of Echinacea in my teeth.

        Everything is water in my hands, he says
for he is alone with the shadow
        of such words, feeling the resurrected blizzard

blow across the weather
of his skull,
a breath that urges everything that's still, everything invisible, vast,

        of no significance, to move through this firmament
of shattered glass,
with names like Cassiopeia on the tongue.

        With his slender arms outstretched
he catches the sun
        in slow motion, mouth open to receive the sorrowful owl at
                                        dusk,

        dung beetle, red-winged blackbird, bunting,
waste of the white-tail grazing in late fall.
Look, he says, I have come to nothing!

4.

UNCLE HARLAN THAT NOVEMBER DAY
and the three of us lie down among scarlet globe mallow,

fringed sage and pasque,
      speaking as though to no one, our spirits intertwined,

    the ants in exodus, the coyote crossing into the valley
       catching our
          scent—lie down
and are united in a single dream of riding the night sky

    that never happened, grave after grave long vanished,
that good meal at twilight,

    that kiss, until we can't tell the three of us apart, are neither
                         there nor here, are elsewhere,
singing:
       *You came into the world      there was a cry*

   *white silence beyond the hospital window*
      *flew*
   *it would be summer    in no time*

   *fall    turn as you might*
      *leaves drifted   smoke gave back its beauty*
   *in great swirls*

   *and the sparrow chased the crow   curved off*
      *wind-driven   you knew what the dark could do*
   *you could see the future   perfectly*

   *it was the present   a man stood up in a boat and laughed*

     *it was the past*

There is a grave for the years of getting up before sunrise
to look for the star
    that flees just east of the Pleiades.

    There is
a coffin within great spaces that are themselves a space, a still point

    moving without seeming to.

    In the beginning what withers is what persists, cryptic signature
of the diamondback,
    fragrance of coneflower. Death no longer death. The dance

        you want comes back: those whirling of arms, those chants.
    Where is it? No matter,
says my father, spinning to dust.

5.

Once,
crossing the Missouri River at dawn

        my father felt the surge of power fail

    and cursed the outboard back into sound
but not before that long interlude of going

        serenely in low tones with the almost
unmoving flow: mirror of my father's cigar

    disfigured—perfectly reformed. I know

        now that moment of talking and gliding
holds us, locked in a sanctuary

        of burning glass,
    to be called back when the odor

             of wet stillness and the memory of childhood
under the morning star
                                come effortlessly together.


                          My father gives up
to light in cupped hands his cigar then sits back


             to inquire into a life no longer mine. In time
        that earnest conversation is lost.
                                And whoever I am is lost.


6.


Tell me,
in what hour of your going forth,
                your going back,
of all your unions,
                in what hour would you take with you


anything less
than this, which couldn't be further from the truth


    and yet is not a lie?


7.


That night when I got on the Ferris wheel illuminated like a halo
on its side and rose over the upturned faces lifting into the wind,
when I knew the elation of looking down at the teenager
tugging on her lover who followed her into the house of horrors,
when I reached the peak and saw on the highway the stream
of headlights and the evening star, a tractor abandoned
for the night on the construction lot, windows in the Hotel Swan,
one with a silhouette watching the aura all around us—
when I descended, catching once more the odor of the elephants,
level with the attendant who turned and spat, drawing his hand
across his mouth, when I stepped back and entered a heaven
of human voices more intimately than ever before and walked

past the sword swallower, the fire-eater, the bearded witch,
the bumper cars sparking and sliding, I could believe the meaning
of the world lay open in my arms: when I looked up
and away at that wheel of light turning against the night.


8.


The sunflower faces east
and is at peace,
visited by supplicants with wings.
Flagellation of stem and petal.
Unknown root. It is as if in slow light
approaching the talus of a precipice
the reassurance you sought
was being sought in you,
ululation of prairie grass, thistle.
November's rigid senility of trees.
Palm on frosted glass.
All are vanished when the heart
stops flashing its black gown
and the long body of Uncle Harlan
is lain out, white shirt, striped tie,
pale lips of the merry prankster
pursed to resist analysis.

Uncle Harlan that November day
and dead leaves whisper. Curtains
whip inward. What do you seek
if not yourself in these pacific eyes
upturned at evening? Shades
of green. Oarlocks creaking.
Nightbirds below the quarter moon.

And then you too look up:
it's dawn and no one's here.
Or you are in a crowd of revelers

on a morning when wind
scented with honeysuckle
yields up the memory of an afternoon
of yellow and crimson wildflowers in a meadow
just south of Redfield.
And the mirth of many dancers fills the air.

9.

I remember how it was in the darkening twilight.
How the sky took on a luster behind the bluffs
just as the sun went down beyond the river.
One idea—that everything falls away, is lost—
shocked me, although I was just a kid looking at a river
throwing a flat rock off the water. You think
all sorts of things when you're a kid looking at a river.
You keep them until the day arrives when you finally
waken into a world you never thought possible: the horizon's
stained scarlet and the long reach of clouds, the wind
beginning to speak forcefully in the cottonwoods. One idea.
Nothing lasts. Not even the silent river at your feet.
Not that first star directly overhead in a firmament
turning light to dark—turning aquamarine.
And you let that truth come at you. You let it sing.

# FIVE

Honor The Cold Wind And The Clear Day

        vast invisibilities of light and darkness,
the four truths of the earth,
        flesh of the martyr coated with tar
    to burn slowly, wood smoke blowing in

        over the city changing to April rain,
the water relentlessly moving,
    the blue flower on the porch,
        the Appaloosa with her gentle *yes*
    cropping grass in late August,

    the silence of night without stars,
morning that endlessly wakens,
    the nun, the night nurse. Honor the winding
        path where the serpent coils, contriver of storms,
    thunder that shakes the house

        for days, the blood-colored sunset
over the gulf off the coast of Florida.
    Taste of salt. The scent, at first confusing,
        coming from the apple trees across the avenue,
grass sprung up in the cracks of mortar,

    this morning's cry of crickets
underneath my window. Skin and scroll.
            The lyrical imitation offered by the mockingbird.
    At the wake for Malcolm Lee, honor the coffin
    and baby carriage inside the door,

    the chalice over which a red spell hovers,
memory, and memory's mole: the close of autumn
    and clean wood cleft by the ax, water,
            the threat of thirst at the back of the mouth,
the first pulse created out of love for what is there

like a hand gone looking for another in the dark.

# Wild Iris, Grass Widow, Brome

But if you decided to lie with me
what might come of your cry
for sunlight caressing meadows of sweet clover,
your need to reach
into streams steered years into some voluptuous tributary?

Night wind still circulates
blackening this valley, as if this might be twilight
and twilight this mystery
of slow wind. Even the dragonfly consents
to this way of seeing
when evening and late afternoon begin to blend.

Come nearer. There leans
on everything a benediction of wings.
Their longing song has come so far and thus upset
what clarified—what was most clear.
I cannot lift a finger for myself.

Then the prayer of the estuary appears,
scented with lilies. It is here,
dark hair spilling, clothed in billowing silk,
where I am learned.
Your one breath trembles the underside of earth.

Close round my only shape
this shadow that stands for solitariness
as yellow stands for love
diagonally ascending the hillside shale.
I cannot move on this prairie.

The Ease Of Immeasurable Things

     Give me once more my love of this long
  witnessed wind
worn down by what's become of me.
  What clings to me,
    clear wings of the dragonfly—night's only shape—
at the altar
    of rose—at the temple of common trillium.

     Give me this wisp
  of desert willow and crimson epilobium,
my way of seeking:
  white-fringed feather blown down on the mind
    absent of people,
consolation of long-necked bluestem, sad-faced heather,
  touched every way—that still meadow
     where shadows sweep out in undulations of lupine.

     And leave me there.
For this mysterious summer knows me
  as seed. As grain.
   What slept there, wept there,
blush of coming when coming seemed so near.
  Give me my need. And leave me there.

    Give me too the dream
  of immeasurable things, larch and aspen, deep needlegrass,
old-faced boulder, the breadth of twilight
  wheeling along the pasture
   so slowly as to seem unmoving
except in my mind, my shadowed sheer cliffs
  of shale. Give willingly and leave

    me broken and changed by this shape
  that justifies my way. Speechless gold-leafed thicket
of thorns go on streaming in May
  where a woman in blue denim wakes, wakes me,
   touched every way,
among dark yellow blossoms
  of my making   of what has become of me.

# Wildfire

                                                  Those are the eyes
of the boy at ten hoarding some precious aspect of himself
after cupping a flame to needlegrass grown parched and purled
in late August. Those are my eyes
scouring uncontrollable fire through meadows
praising endlessly, unfurling along a ditch as if this were all there is

for the kid at thirteen breathlessly remembering what God wants.
Believe in what is seen. In what is being dreamed,
wildfire, turning east,
skirting that childish mind that will go on thinking indefinitely
*nightmare of ash, thirst that makes fire*
*more than fire.* Fire the metaphor for everything.

# To The Living Wind

Cattle in cold wind. Then crows floating
over the stubble field—a stake
being driven into the earth by a man
with nothing but answers in his hands.

I have studied the possibilities and I know
if sweet clover turned black in the middle
of May and the fox responded to prayer
the day would still contain the uncontrollable

sound of someone lifting and pulling—
long after the sun topped the buttes—
a sledgehammer with such force
you would think a fissure had opened up in the loam

letting go the dead. Go out over the fields. Go alone.
This is your history. This is where you begin.

History

Never to lie down again with my sisters in the middle of August
        in a field, listening for that train that comes
        once a day outside Pierre, South Dakota
Never to turn away from the Great Dane Bones
        eaten thin with cancer, at the veterinarian's,
        the injection beginning to work and the look
        of absolute abandonment on his too-human face
Never to sense the presence of those dark downward-gazing eyes
        and the dispassionate lifting of the head
        as I wrote in the light of the kitchen lamp
        and someone I loved called out
Never to reach up, switch off the light, sit quietly
        thinking of my old mother, her fingers twisted
        and swollen with arthritis—of my father's obsession
        with the lawn, on his back those folds of skin
Never to climb again that long ladder as the sun was coming
        up above the high-rises in windless October,
        stepping out onto the roof slick with frost
        until the sun healed me and I backed down,
        shaken by how close I had come
        to flying backward into the arms of the air
Never to stand in a circle of men saying nothing,
        their fingers black from tightening the bolts
        of a winch engine, their soft eyes lifting
        when one of them speaks of a life that has to get better
Or to enter that white house again beside a white meadow
        with someone near, the light on
        outside on the porch, already whirling with insects
Just to sleep, and to sleep deeply, without disturbance
        at the end of a day that waits for me on the other side
        of the world
        with the understanding that there is no life but this.